PURPLE AND SPOTTY JOKE BOOK

Also available from Mammoth

The Biodegradable Joke Book
The Creepy Crawly Joke Book
My Funny Valentine
The Green and Hairy Joke Book
The Holiday Joke Book
Love and Kisses
The Pink and Wobbly Joke Book
The Yellow and Highly Dangerous Joke Book

THE PURPLE AND SPOTTY JOKE BOOK

Logan Berry

Illustrated by Tony Blundell

MAMMOTH

Published 1991 by Mammoth
an imprint of Mandarin Paperbacks
Michelin House, 81 Fulham Road, London SW3 6RB

Mandarin is an imprint of the Octopus Publishing Group

ISBN 0 7497 0614 7

A CIP catalogue record for this title
is available from the British Library

Printed in Great Britain
by Cox & Wyman Ltd, Reading, Berkshire

What's purple and spotty?
A plum with measles.

Why do plums always forget?
What do they have to remember?

What's purple and spotty and drinks from the wrong side of the glass?
A plum with measles and hiccups.

What do you call a plum that is green and skinny at harvest time?
A failure.

What's purple and spotty and coughs?
A plum with measles and a bad chest.

How were Humpty Dumpty and the plum with a weak stem alike?
They both had a great fall.

What do you get if you cross two plums with a banana skin?
A pair of purple slippers.

Why wouldn't the ripe plum sit on the wall?
It had heard what happened to Humpty Dumpty.

What do you have when 2,000 plums try to get through a door together?
Plum jam.

What's purple and spotty and goes bang?
A plum with measles in a minefield.

What's purple and spotty and takes aspirins?
A plum with measles and a headache.

What does a plum do when it's raining?
Gets wet.

Why did the girl plum dye her hair yellow?
To see if blondes have more fun.

How can you tell a plum from an elephant?
A plum always forgets.

What did the plum say to the greenfly?
You really bug me.

What's the difference between a plum and a worm?
Ever tried eating worm pie?

What do you get if you cross a plum with an elephant?
Fruit that never forgets.

What do you get if you cross the M1 with a plum?
Run over!

What's a good way of putting on weight?
Eat a plum, swallow the centre, and you've gained a stone.

What family does the plum belong to?
I don't know, nobody in our street has one.

What did the Ribena say to the water?
Diluted to meet you.

Knock knock.
Who's there?
Orange.
Orange who?
Orange you glad I didn't say plum!

BOY: This Ribena is terrible.
FATHER: I made it in my pyjamas.
BOY: No wonder it tastes so bad.

What do you get if you cross a plum with an alligator?
Fruit that bites back.

What sort of tea makes you feel brave?
Safety.

What do you call a man who can sing and drink lemonade at the same time?
A pop singer.

What do you get if you cross a bottle of lemonade with Orville?
Duck's Fizz.

How do you make ginger wine?
Twist his arm up his back.

What did one chick say to the other chick when it found an orange in the nest?
Look at the orange mama laid!

What do you get if you cross an orange with a bell?
An orange that can peal itself.

Why did the orange go to the doctor?
Because it wasn't peeling well.

What's wet and comes out of a bottle at 100mph?
An Aston Martini.

Knock knock.
Who's there?
Plum.
Plum who?
Knock knock.
Who's there?
Plum.
Plum who?
Knock knock.
Who's there?
Plum.
Plum who???
Knock knock.
Who's there?
Orange.
Orange who?
Orange you glad I didn't say plum!

How is a plum like a wise man?
Neither reads the Sun.

What did the green plum say to the blue plum?
Cheer up!

What do you get if you cross a bottle of lemonade with a masseur?
A fizzy o'therapist.

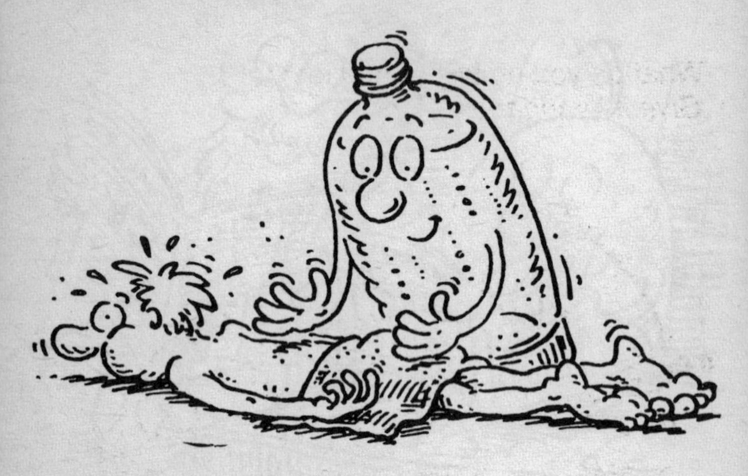

What do little devils drink?
Demonade.

What did the orange say to the other orange on the telephone?
Nothing, the pips went!

What do you do with a hurt lemon?
Give it lemonade.

Why couldn't the orange get up the hill?
Because it had run out of juice.

What does a vegetarian vampire eat?
Blood oranges.

What do you get when you cross an orange and a squash court?
Orange squash.

What is square and green?
A lemon in disguise.

What was the orange doing in a palm tree?
It had heard that coconuts have more fun.

What is the difference between a lemon and a melon?
The order in which their letters are written.

What is a tangerine?
An orange in an easy-open wrapper.

What's purple and highly dangerous?
Shark-infested Ribena.

Where do the world's biggest plums come from?
The world's biggest plum trees.

What's purple on top, has four legs and a tail, and whinnies?
A plum on horseback.

What is the best way to keep plums?
Don't return them.

What did one plum say to the other plum?
Nothing. Plums can't talk.

Who is purple, rides a motorbike, and jumps over buses?
Evel Plumevel.

What was the smallest plum?
Tom Plum.

What did the dentist say when his wife baked a plum pie?
Can I do the filling?

Why is a Boy Scout like a tin of plums?
They are both prepared.

Where do you find wild plums?
It depends where they were lost.

What's red and clings to metal?
A magnetic tomato.

If your cat ate an unripe plum, what would she become?
A sourpuss.

What's round, red and cheeky?
Tomato sauce.

What can a whole red tomato do but half a red tomato can't?
Look round.

What's purple and spotty and wears sunglasses?
A plum with measles and a black eye.

Why did the tomato go red?
Because it saw the salad dressing.

Why was the tomato in such a hurry?
It wanted to ketchup (catch up).

Why does a plum make a good museum keeper?
Plum preserves.

There were two tomatoes on horseback. Which was the cowboy?
Neither – they were both redskins.

Why did the man have to go to hospital after the blackcurrant jam fell on his head?
It was in a jar.

A man saw a gardener pushing a wheel-barrow full of manure.
'Where are you going with that?' he asked.
'Going to put it on my blackcurrants,' said the gardener.
'Suit yourself,' said the man. 'I usually put sugar and cream on mine!'

1ST GIRL: Here, try some of this blackcurrant jam I've just made.
2ND GIRL: Ugh! It's horrible!
1ST GIRL: You've no taste – it definitely says in my cookery book that this recipe is delicious.

What should you do if your pet plum falls ill?
Call the plumber.

What's yellow on the outside and purple on the inside?
A plum disguised as an apricot.

What's purple and hard and wears dark glasses?
A jar of blackcurrant jam in disguise.

What happened to West Brom-witch Albion?
They had a spell in the first division.

Have you heard about the weather witch?
She's forecasting sunny spells.

What's purple and warty and smells?
A witch's nose.

What happens to a witch when she loses her temper?
She flies off the handle.

What's purple and hard and wears sunglasses?
A jar of blackcurrant jam on holiday.

What's purple and hard and moves along the bottom of the sea?
A jar of blackcurrant jam in a submarine.

What's purple and hard and has four wheels?
A jar of blackcurrant jam on a skateboard.

What's purple and hard and has eight wheels?
A jar of blackcurrant jam on roller skates.

Two witches came out of the theatre one night. One said to the other, 'Shall we walk home, or shall we take a broom?'

What happened to the naughty witch schoolgirl?
She was ex-spelled.

Why do witches get good bargains?
Because they like to haggle.

What are baby witches called?
Halloweenies.

What do you call two witches who share a broom?
Broom-mates.

What's the best thing to do with a green alien?
Wait until he's ripe.

What's purple and slimy and goes up and down?
An alien in a lift.

What has three purple eyes like an alien, an arm like an alien, four hands like an alien, but isn't an alien?
A photograph of an alien.

What happens if you are confronted with two identical hags?
You can't tell witch is witch.

Why did the witch put her broom in the washing machine?
She wanted a clean sweep.

LITTLE BOY TO PARROT IN ZOO: Say little birdie, can you talk?
PARROT: Yes, can you fly?

What do you get if you cross a parrot with a homing pigeon?
A bird that asks its way home if it gets lost.

Why can't you find aspirins in the jungle?
Because the parrots eat 'em all!

What did the astronaut say about the ten-legged aliens?
Don't worry, they're armless.

ALIEN TO HIS FRIEND: What's that ugly purple thing on your neck? Oh sorry, it's your head!

What do you get if you cross a parrot with a soldier?
A parrot-trooper.

What's purple and slimy and travels at 100mph?
An alien on a motorbike.

What singing birds come from Cornwall?
The Parrots of Penzance.

Did you hear about the scientist who crossed a parrot with a crocodile?
It bit off his arm and said, 'Who's a pretty boy then?'

TEACHER: What is a polygon?
PUPIL: An empty parrot cage, Miss.

A purple and slimy alien was travelling by himself in his spaceship. As he hovered over a farm, he called down to the farmer: 'Hallo, Earthling. Where am I?' The farmer looked up. 'You can't fool me,' he shouted. 'You're up there in that little spaceship!'

What happens when aliens hold a beauty contest?
Nobody wins.

Who is safe when a man-eating leopard is loose?
Women and children.

Where do you find leopards?
It depends where you lost them.

Who would win a fight between an African lion and an African tiger?
Neither – there aren't any tigers in Africa.

When should you feed leopard's milk to a baby?
When it's a baby leopard.

Did you hear about the man who bought his mother a very rare parrot for her birthday? It could speak ten languages, play chess, and sing the entire works of Mozart. He asked her what she thought of the bird.
'It was delicious, son,' she said, 'absolutely delicious . . .'

When is a man-eating leopard most likely to enter your house?
When the door is open.

What do you get if you cross a plum with a leopard?
A highly dangerous purple people-eater.

What do you stuff dead parrots with?
Polyfilla.

What do you get if you cross a fierce leopard with Father Christmas?
Santa Claws.

A leopard was about to eat a missionary. It had the man cornered, but suddenly fell down on its knees and started to pray.
'It's a miracle!' cried the missionary. 'I'm saved! The tiger isn't going to eat me after all.'
Just then, a heavenly voice boomed down. 'You're wrong,' it said, 'he *is* going to eat you. But first, he's saying his grace.'

What is a Macaw?
A Scottish parrot.

Why shouldn't you pull a leopard by his tail?
It may only be his tail, but it could be your end.

What did the idiot call his pet tiger?
Spot!

ZOOKEEPER: I've just crossed a hyena with a leopard.
ASSISTANT: What did you get?
ZOOKEEPER: I don't know, but when it laughs you'd better join in.

What do French people eat for breakfast?
Huit heures bix!

What's purple and French and writes under an assumed name?
Nom de plum.

What would you get if all the cars in France were purple?
A purple carnation.

What do you get if you cross the Channel with a sailing ship?
To the other side.

What's a guillotine?
A French chopping centre.

What's 300 metres tall, weighs 7,620 tons and attracts bees?
The Eiffel Flower.

What's wrapped in cling-film and terrorises Paris?
The lunch-pack of Notre Dame.

What's the quickest way to the Gard du Nord station?
Run as fast as you can.

What's purple and spotty?
A grape that eats too much chocolate.

What's made of chocolate and rolls along the seabed?
An oyster egg.

What's woolly, covered in chocolate, and floats around the sun?
A Mars baaa.

What's clever, made of chocolate and travels by underground?
A Tube of Smarties.

What did the chocolate say to the lollipop?
Hi, sucker.

What do you call a girl that's covered in chocolate?
Candy.

What do you get if you cross an elk with a packet of cocoa?
Chocolate moose.

What's purple and yellow and green, with a twenty-metre wingspan?
A two-ton parrot.

TEACHER: Where did Captain Cook stand when he discovered Australia?
PUPIL: On his feet.

TEACHER: Did you know that Columbus found America?
PUPIL: I didn't even know it was lost.

What do you get if you cross a chocolate with a madman?
A coconut.

Who was purple and discovered America in 1492?
Christopher Plumbus.

Who sailed around Ireland and invented mints?
Marc O'Polo.

TEACHER: On what date did Columbus cross the Atlantic?
PUPIL: He didn't cross on a date, he crossed on a ship.

What did the cannibal say when he met the famous explorer?
Doctor Livingstone, I consume?

What do you get if you cross eight arms with a watch?
A clocktopus.

What's wet and says 'How do you do?' sixteen times?
Two octopuses shaking hands.

What makes an octopus a very good fighter?
He is well-armed.

What bus sailed the ocean?
Columbus.

Which ghost discovered America?
Christopher Ghoulumbus.

What lives under the sea and carries 64 people?
An octobus.

Who snatched the baby octopus and held it to ransom?
Squidnappers.

Why did the man cross a chicken with an octopus?
So his family could have a leg each.

Who was round and purple and ruled Russia?
Peter the Grape.

What's purple and has eight legs?
An octoplum.

IGOR: Why is Baron Frankenstein such good fun?
MONSTER: Because he soon has you in stitches!

Why was Baron Frankenstein never lonely?
Because he was good at making friends.

What do you call a neurotic octopus?
A crazy mixed-up squid.

1ST MONSTER: The bride of Frankenstein has a lovely face.
2ND MONSTER: If you can read between the lines.

What did Frankenstein's monster say when he was struck by lightning?
Great! That was just what I needed.

Did you hear what happened to Frankenstein's monster?
He was stopped for speeding, fined £50, and dismantled for six months.

Who is purple, has scars on his head, and frightens people?
Frankenplum.

What do you call a clever monster?
Frank Einstein.

What does Frankenstein's monster call a screwdriver?
Daddy.

What is written on the grave of Frankenstein's monster?
Rust in peace.

Who brings the monsters their babies?
Frankenstork.

How did Frankenstein's monster eat his lunch?
He bolted it down.

Who conquered half the world, laying eggs along the way?
Attila the Hen.

Where did the Vikings drink?
At Norse troughs.

Who led hordes of fighting convent girls?
Attila the Nun.

Who was Russia's greatest gardener?
Ivan-hoe!

Who was full of hay and conquered Mongolia?
Ghengis Barn.

A diner in a restaurant asked the waitress what flavours of ice cream were on the menu. The waitress answered in a very hoarse whisper: 'Vanilla, chocolate, and blackcurrant.' Sympathising with her condition, the man asked: 'Do you have laryngitis?' 'No,' croaked the waitress, 'just the vanilla, chocolate and blackcurrant.'

What do you get if you cross an invader with a cake?
Attila the Bun.

How did the Vikings communicate with each other?
By Norse code.

Which cyclist defeated the Spanish Armada?
Sir Francis Trike.

Two ants were in a supermarket. They climbed up on a shelf and on to a box containing a blackcurrant pie. Suddenly the first ant began running.
'Wait for me', cried the other ant. 'What's the hurry?'
'Can't you read?' said the first. 'It says here: TEAR ALONG THE DOTTED LINE.'

What's purple and wobbles in the sky?
A blackcurrant jelly-copter.

MAN IN RESTAURANT: Will you join me in a piece of blackcurrant pie?
WOMAN: Do you think there's room for both of us?

Why did the blackberry jelly wobble?
Because it saw the milk shake.

What's big and wobbly, and fights crime?
Jelly Savalas.

What's small and wobbly and sits in a pram?
A jelly-baby.

Why are blackcurrant seeds like gateposts?
Because they propagate.

What is purple, has one bionic eye, and fights crime?
The Six Million Dollar Aubergine.

How many aubergines can you put into an empty sack?
One. After that the sack is no longer empty.

What's purple and wobbles in the corner of your living-room?
A blackcurrant jelly-vision.

What wobbles on a pile of blancmange in the middle of Paris?
The Trifle Tower.

What are you if you've got a blancmange in one ear, and a jelly in the other?
A trifle deaf.

What did one aubergine say to the other aubergine?
Take me to your weeder.

What is purple and goes putt, putt?
An outboard aubergine.

What's purple and comes out of the ground at 100mph?
An E-type aubergine.

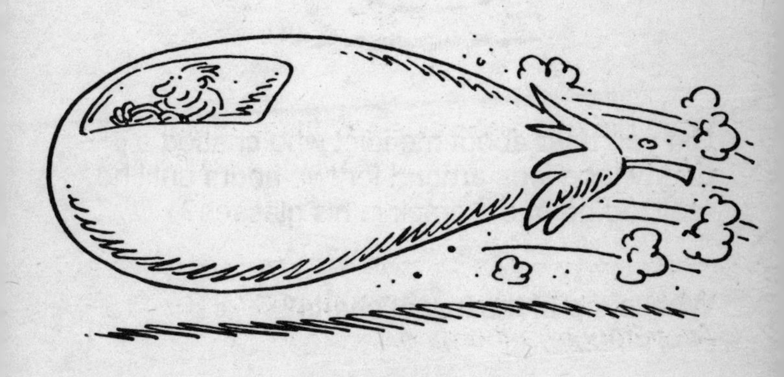

How do you tell the good aubergines from the bad ones?
The good aubergines have haloes.

Did you hear about the idiot who chased a daddy long legs around for two hours until he realized he had a crack in his glasses?

Who is top of the insect charts?
Bug's Fizz.

Why did the baby aubergine colour itself orange?
So it could hide in the carrot patch.

Knock, knock.
Who's there?
Weevil.
Weevil who?
Weevil work it out.

CUSTOMER: Waiter, there's a cockroach in my soup!
WAITER: Yes sir, the fly is on holiday.

What's purple and spotty and flies badly?
A ladybird with a bruised back.

What goes 99-klonk, 99-klonk, 99-klonk?
A centipede with a wooden leg.

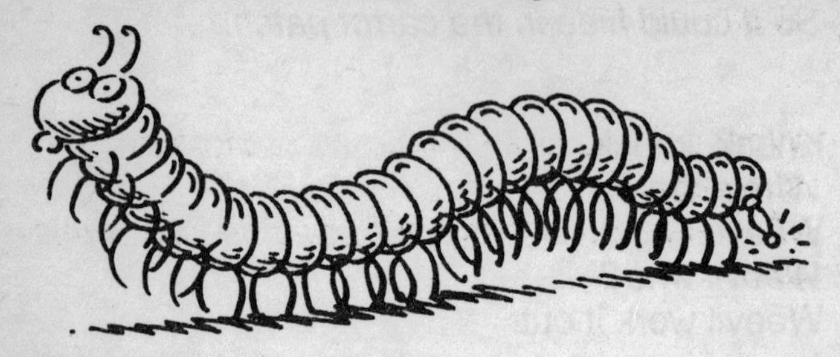

What is red, has bumps and a horse, and lives on the prairie?
The Lone Raspberry.

What do you get when you cross an apple with a Christmas tree?
A pineapple.

What did one strawberry say to the other strawberry?
Between you and me, we shouldn't be in this jam.

Did you hear about the idiot caterpillar?
It turned into a frog!

Why did the baby strawberry cry?
Because his mother was in a jam.

What did the girl say after she ate a basket of fresh plums?
Burp!

What is rhubarb?
Celery with high blood pressure.

When insects take a trip, how do they travel?
In a buggy.

Which famous Norseman sailed the Atlantic a thousand years ago?
Eric the Red Apple.

What do farmers do to endangered strawberries?
Put them in preserves.

Did you hear the story about the world's biggest strawberry?
Never mind, it's over your head.

Who was purple and burnt the cakes?
Alfred the Grape.

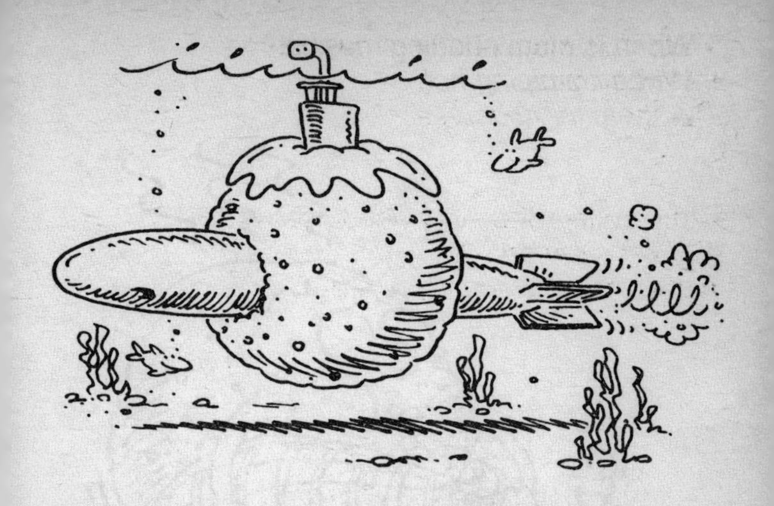

What's purple and steaming and travels along the seabed?
A plum pudding in a submarine.

Why is plum pudding like the sea?
Because it's full of currants.

What's purple and steaming and goes up and down?
A plum pudding in a lift.

What's purple and steaming and goes slam-slam-slam-slam?
A four-door plum pudding.

When is plum pudding musical?
When it's piping hot.

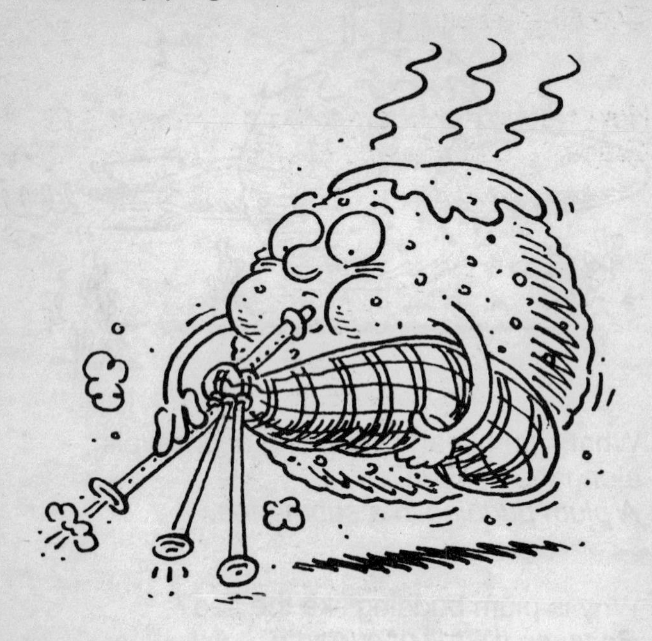

BOY: I don't like this plum pudding.
WOMAN: Oh, don't you? I'll have you know I was making plum puddings before you were born.
BOY: Perhaps this is one of them.

What is the best thing to put into plum pudding?
Your teeth.

What American lakes are filled with purple juice?
The Grape Lakes.

How can you tell a grape from an aspirin?
Grapes are purple and come in bunches.

MAN: This plum pudding is nice and warm.
WOMAN: It should be – the cat's been sitting on it.

What's purple, washable, dries quickly and needs no ironing?
A drip-dry grape.

Why don't grapes have dandruff?
Did you ever see a grape with hair?

Why didn't the grape snore?
Because it was afraid of waking up the rest of the bunch.

Why did the grape go to the doctor?
Because it wasn't peeling very well?

What's purple and round and floats in space?
The Planet of the Grapes.

Who was purple and ruled the world?
Alexander the Grape.

What did the grape say when the elephant trod on it?
Nothing – it just gave out a little wine.

What's purple and steaming and comes at you from all sides?
Stereophonic plum pudding.

What do you get if you cross an aubergine with a skunk?
A skunk with a purple streak down its back.

What's purple and goes 'Beep, beep'?
An aubergine in a traffic jam.

What was the film where 100 grapes tunnelled out of the prisoner-of-war camp?
The Grape Escape.

Why can't an aubergine be twelve inches long?
Because then it would be a foot.

Why don't aubergines worry when people say nasty things about them?
Aubergines are noted for their thick skins.

TEACHER: How do you spell 'aubergine'?
PUPIL: O-b-e-r-j-e-a-n.
TEACHER: The dictionary spells it a-u-b-e-r-g-i-n-e.
PUPIL: You didn't ask me how the dictionary *spells it!*

What's purple and good at sums?
An aubergine with a calculator.

TEACHER: If I had eight aubergines in one hand, and six in the other, what would I have?
PUPIL: Big hands.

What's long and purple and red all over?
An embarrassed aubergine.

SHERLOCK HOLMES: Ah, Watson, you are wearing your purple thermal underpants today . . .
DR WATSON: Absolutely astounding, Holmes! How on earth did you deduce that?
SHERLOCK HOLMES: Elementary, my dear Watson. You forgot to put your trousers on.

What's long and purple and goes 'hith'?
A purple snake with a lisp.

That's a strange pair of socks you've got on – one dark purple and one light purple.
I know – I've got another pair just like it at home.

What's big and purple and lives in Scotland?
The Loch Ness Aubergine.

What's purple and points north?
A magnetic aubergine.

What is an aubergine skin most used for?
To keep the aubergine together.

What's purple and points south?
A stupid magnetic aubergine.

What is purple and runs in slow motion?
The Bionic Nose.

What's purple and goes thump-squish, thump-squish?
An aubergine with one wet plimsoll.

Why don't they grow aubergines any longer?
Because they're long enough already.

How do you stop a herd of aubergines from charging?
Take away their credit cards.

What do purple cabbages use for stockings?
Garden hose.

What is the hardest thing to eat?
An aubergine sideways.

What's long and purple and roars around the vegetable patch at 60mph?
An aubergine on a motorbike.

Why was the purple cabbage disliked by all the other vegetables?
It had a big head.

What's purple and close to France?
Grape Britain.

How did the purple cabbage talk to the green cabbage?
Head to head.

How can you find the most attractive purple cabbage in the patch?
She's the one with the most boyfriends.

Why didn't the boy eat his purple cabbage after his mother told him it would put colour in his cheeks?
He didn't want purple cheeks.

Why are purple cabbages so generous?
Because they have big hearts.

What happened to the criminal prune?
It was taken into custardy.

What's purple and curly and jumps up and down?
A purple cabbage at a disco.

Where can you find aubergines, potatoes, broccoli and swedes, no matter what time of the year it is?
In the dictionary.

LADY (to a tramp who's asked for a meal): Do you like cold prunes and custard?
TRAMP: I love it, lady.
LADY: Well call back later, it's very hot right now.

How can you tell an apple from a purple cabbage?
If it's red it's probably an apple.

What's green and red and purple and spins round at 100mph?
Kermit eating grapes in a liquidizer.

Why did the police arrest the purple cabbage?
It was involved in a garden plot.

Why did the grape go out with the prune?
Because he couldn't find a date.

What do you get if you cross a grape with a comedian?
Peels of laughter.

What do you get if you cross a bowl of prunes and custard with a pair of roller skates?
Meals on wheels.

What's purple and lumpy and wears sunglasses?
Prunes and custard on holiday.

What's red outside, purple and yellow inside, and very crowded?
A bus full of prunes and custard.

What's purple and lumpy inside and white outside?
A prunes and custard sandwich.

What's purple, covered in custard, and miserable?
Plum grumble.

Why did the man have to go to hospital after the prune fell on his head?
It was in a tin.

What's purple and highly dangerous?
A bunch of stampeding grapes.

What's purple and glows in the dark?
A 100 watt grape.

What's purple and barks at people?
A Grape Dane.

Who swings through the vines?
Tarzan of the Grapes.

What's purple and lumpy and goes round and round?
Prunes and custard in a revolving door.

What's purple and highly dangerous?
A bunch of angry grapes.

If you have a referee in boxing, a referee in football, and a referee in rugby, what do you have in bowls?
Prunes and custard.

What's purple and 8,000 kilometres long?
The Grape Wall of China.

What's purple and ruled Russia?
Catherine the Grape.

What do you get when you cross a grape with a chicken?
A hen that lays bunches of purple eggs.

What's purple has four wheels and is used in wine making?
Grapes – I lied about the wheels.

What's green and hairy on the outside, and purple on the inside?
A grape disguised as a gooseberry.

Why are grapes never lonely?
Because they hang around in bushes.